Our Bodies

Our Lungs

Charlotte Guillain

www.heinemannlibrary.co.uk
Visit our website to find out more information about Heinemann Library books.

To order:
☎ Phone +44 (0) 1865 888066
🖹 Fax +44 (0) 1865 314091
🖳 Visit www.heinemannlibrary.co.uk

Heinemann Library is an imprint of Capstone Global Library Limited, a company incorporated in England and Wales having its registered office at 7 Pilgrim Street, London, EC4V 6LB – Registered company number: 6695582

Heinemann is a registered trademark of Pearson Education Limited, under licence to Capstone Global Library Limited

Text © Capstone Global Library Limited 2010
First published in hardback in 2010
The moral rights of the proprietor have been asserted.

Edited by Siân Smith, Laura Knowles, Nancy Dickmann, and Rebecca Rissman
Designed by Joanna Hinton-Malivoire
Original Illustrations © Capstone Global Library Ltd. 2010
Illustrated by Tony Wilson
Picture research by Ruth Blair and Mica Brancic
Production by Duncan Gilbert and Victoria Fitzgerald
Originated by Capstone Global Library Ltd
Printed and bound in China by Leo Paper Group

ISBN 978 0 431 19505 6
14 13 12 11 10
10 9 8 7 6 5 4 3 2 1

British Library Cataloguing in Publication Data
Guillain, Charlotte.
  Our lungs. -- (Acorn. Our bodies)
  1. Lungs--Juvenile literature.
  I. Title II. Series
  612.2-dc22

Acknowledgements
We would like to thank the following for permission to reproduce photographs: Corbis pp.**4**, **22** (© John Fortunato Photography), **16**, **23** (© moodboard), **17** (© Image Source), **18** (© Sven Hagolani/zefa); iStockphoto pp.**8**, **9**, **20**; Photolibrary pp.**5** (© Image Source), **15**, **23** (© Goodshoot), **19** (© Flirt Collection); Science Photo Library pp.**12** (© Eye Of Science), **13**, **23** (© Martin Dohrn/ Royal College of Surgeons), **14** (© Coneyl Jay), **21** (© Ian Hooton).

Front cover photograph of a brother and sister playing football reproduced with permission of Corbis (© HBSS). Back cover photograph reproduced with permission of Photolibrary (© Goodshoot).

Every effort has been made to contact copyright holders of material reproduced in this book. Any omissions will be rectified in subsequent printings if notice is given to the publishers.

Contents

Body parts

Our bodies have many parts.

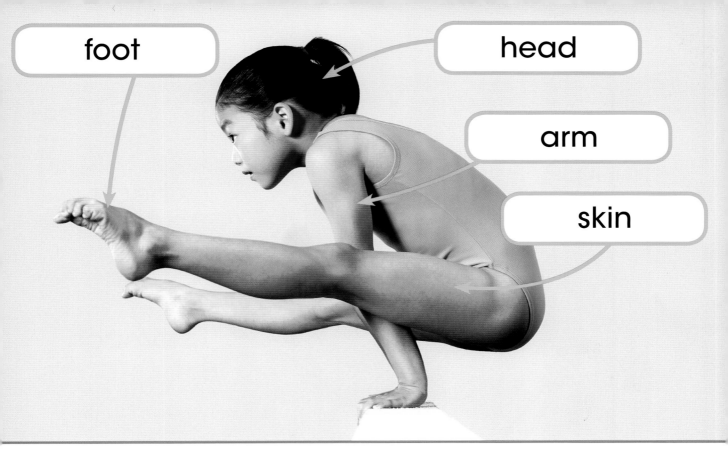

foot

head

arm

skin

Our bodies have parts on the outside.

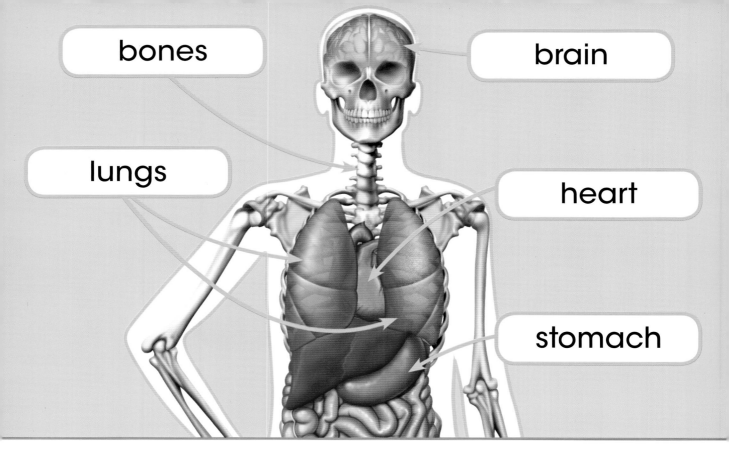

bones

brain

lungs

heart

stomach

Our bodies have parts on
the inside.

lungs

Your lungs are inside your body.

Your lungs

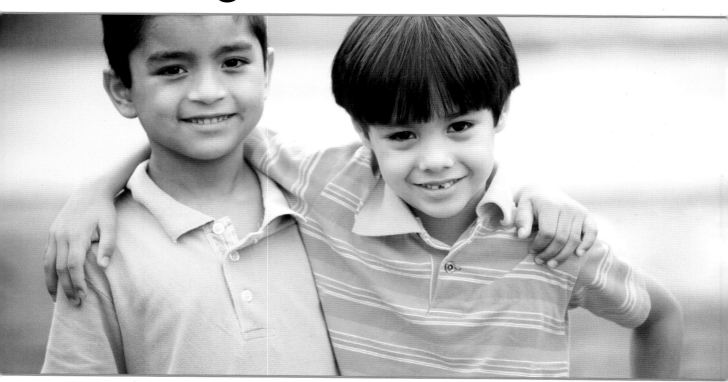

You cannot see your lungs.

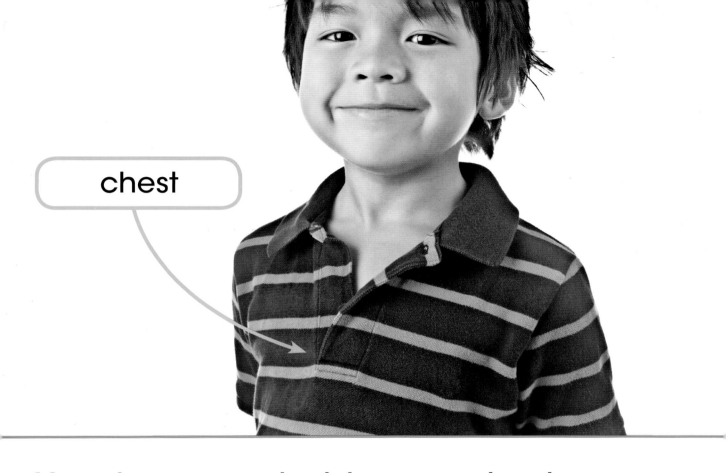

chest

Your lungs are inside your chest.

lungs

You have two lungs in your chest.

bones

Your bones keep your lungs safe.

inside a lung

Your lungs are soft, like a sponge.

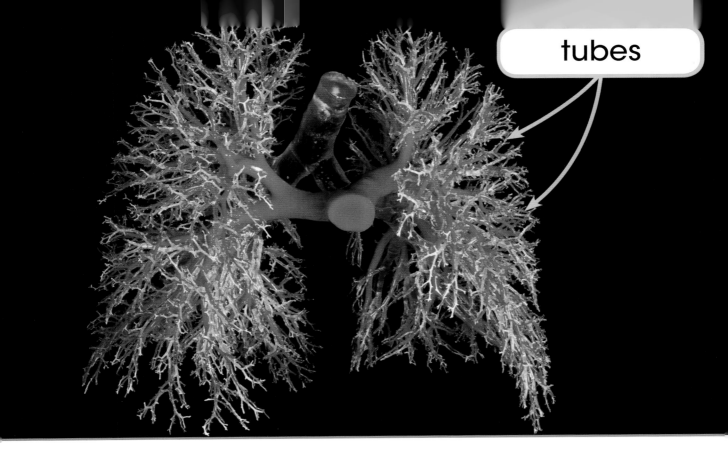

tubes

Your lungs are full of tiny tubes.

Breathing

You can feel your lungs move.

You can feel your lungs breathe in
and out.

Your lungs breathe in air.

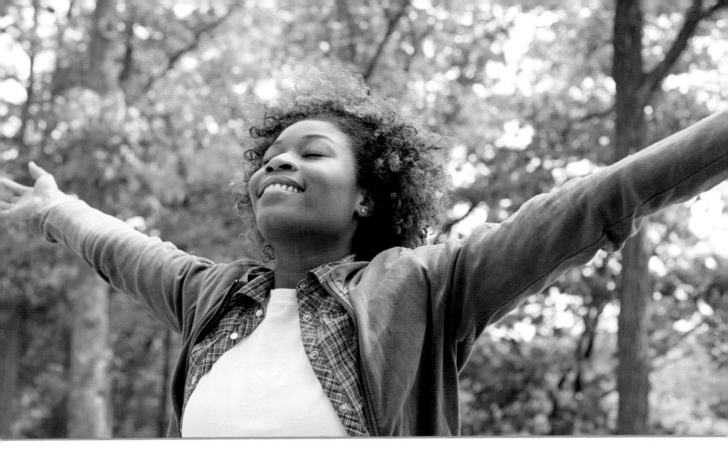

Your need air to live.

Fast and slow

When you are still your lungs
breathe slowly.

When you run your lungs
breathe fast.

Staying healthy

Smoking can hurt your lungs.

Exercise can help your lungs.

Quiz

Where in your body are your lungs?

Answer on page 24

Picture glossary

 air we need to breathe air in to stay alive. Air is all around us but we cannot see it.

 breathe take in air

 lungs parts of your body that help you breathe. You have two lungs inside your chest.

 tube a long, thin pipe like a hose. Things can move along inside tubes because they have an empty space in the middle.

Index

Answer to quiz on page 22: Your lungs are in your chest.

Notes to parents and teachers

Before reading

Ask the children to name the parts of their body they can see on the outside. Then ask them what parts of their body are inside. Make a list of them together and see if the children know what each body part does, for example, food goes into their stomachs. Discuss where their lungs are and see if anyone knows what our lungs do.

After reading

• Take the children outside and ask them to notice how they are breathing. Then tell them to run around for five minutes. When they stop, ask them to think again about how they are breathing. What do they notice?

• Talk to the children about how smoking can damage our lungs and other parts of our bodies. Discuss what they can do to help their lungs stay healthy.